CW01095327

THE BOOK OF TORN UP SUICIDE NOTES

By

Dolly Sen

Hole Books, London

THE BOOK OF TORN UP SUICIDE NOTES

©Dolly Sen 2002

Cover Design © Dolly Sen

ISBN 0-9541837-5-4

The moral right of the author has been asserted

Published by

Hole Books
2 Hailsham Avenue
London, SW2

Q

Dinner queue in the psych ward
I'm stuck between 2 Jesuses
I can see they're both contemplating
feeding the 5 thousand by doing a
miracle of multiplication with the
rubbery macaroni cheese
A schizophrenic soul abuses
any god that is listening
The catatonic philosophises
with empty words
The anorexic looks down her
nose at us for indulging in
the depravity of sustenance
Why am I here?
Reality, sanity is a book of
lies, I've lost my page
I've become celestially illiterate
Because I know the ending – no
happily ever after
just lonely death
following
a life
that is just a queue
waiting, waiting
for the
madness to end

THE PARK BENCH

Everyone's a fucking philosopher.

But there's not much else to do sitting on a park bench.

And you can always tell where the most prolific philosophers sit to chew the fat. The rickety benches they preside over are cordoned off from public use by a circlet of rusting lager empties.

The way I see it: how can you philosophise and not drink yourself stupid after?

Philosophy: the investigation of the nature of being – an ultimately boring and futile subject – but it does help to pass the time.

Shithead, my fellow drinker/thinker, said philosophy is the wisdom of fools. Pretty deep, huh? As deep as the shit we are all in.

"What's the use of a philosophy degree?" Shithead once bemoaned, "It's bloody useless, in it? I mean, it doesn't pay the bills, and there is no world peace because of it, right?"

"I guess you're right," I agreed tepidly.

"Of course I'm right. Learning about philosophy is like learning to swim in set concrete."

Shithead and I discussed and argued and criticised all sorts of theories as much as our diminishing sobriety would allow. Maybe it is the drink that influences my only solid conclusion: my only handy household hint in dealing with onthological insecurity is: stay pissed. Shithead agrees with me wholeheartedly.

Why is Shithead called Shithead? Now that is an easy question to answer. I – and most of our mutual confederates – called him Shithead because that was what he was. It wasn't meant in a derogative sense – he was called much worse by the two beautiful people who brought him into this world. It was an affectionate term because we wanted to call him much worse but didn't. According to reliable sources, Shithead was one odoriferous bastard – an unblocked toilet was a bed of roses compared. When tramps and winos comment disparagingly on someone else's body odour... fucking hell... I wouldn't know personally, mind you – I lost my sense of smell through repeated punches to the nose. I think that was why we were best mates, what with me being the only person able to physically sit next to him. He smelled like shit and looked like shit. If you placed one of those plastic red lips and a fucked up, moth-eaten blond wig on a pile of shit, you'd get a fair resemblance of the human being he is. But he is an okay kind of shit... most of the time.

But inevitably the more you drink, the more of an obnoxious megalomaniac you become: you become critical of everyone and everything. You begin to think everyone is an arsehole except for you. Which is bullshit, of course. Everyone in the world is an arsehole including yourself.

Shithead is in one of those moods right now. There's supposed to be a tentative camaraderie between drunks, which is crap. It's just that we're so pissed we can't be arsed to get up and move on.

Shithead is telling me why he chooses not to be part of society. I'm not really listening; I am more intrigued by the fact that a strand of dried egg yolk in his stubble is turning green.

"If you don't make yourself available to duplicity," he went on, "society loses interest in you, it has no use for you. And you will notice if it has no use for you, you worth goes down. For example, a customer who knows the cons and psychological tricks of an unscrupulous salesperson and isn't taken in by them loses his worth in the eyes of the salesperson. That insincere smile begins to twitch and the welcoming open arms want to beat the shit out of you..."

I sit there and listen to him ramble interminably on. Thank God I only have limited access to full consciousness at the moment, which is a help in any situation, which is a fucking lifesaver, actually.

"All women are whores," Was now the subject of his morbid attention.

Here we go again, I thought.

"Why are all the women I go out with whores?"

"Maybe you specifically pick whorish women to go out with so you can say all women are whores."

"What the fuck are you on about?"

"I dunno," I shrug, unsuspectingly influenced by the fact that I had been reading psychology books all day yesterday in the library because it had been raining.

"Anyway, me last bird used to complain that I came too early while she had only started to get going. 'How would you like to have sex without coming every time?' she asked me.

I conceded she had a point there. So they next time I fucked her I thought unsexy thoughts: I imagined I was fucking Bernard Manning, but I found that strangely arousing. So I dreamed of Barbara Cartland instead. Mission accomplished! When I felt my woman coming, I let go too. But me bird was still complaining! This time she moaned, 'What, I don't turn you on any more? You don't fancy me enough to prematurely ejaculate!' God, there is no pleasing some women."

"You talk a lot of shit sometimes,"

"Why, thank you, Jonno,"

He resumed his diatribe, on which subject I wouldn't know; my weak attention was focused on the clouds sliding across the skies. Sometimes my view of the clouds was interrupted by nightmarish images, horrible, horrible things – human faces. Thankfully they didn't come too close. Actually, people ambling on the path passing our bench would deviate substantially from their route when they approached us; they would rather get their shoes muddy than be in close proximity to us. They either look down on us or try their best not to look at all. Usually they don't say anything, but when they do I either ignore them or chase them across the churchyard swearing that I'm going to chew their goolies off like any good philosopher would.

The general public look upon us with gargoyle expressions of fear, disgust and contempt. I used to get hurt by it, but the consumption of more alcohol wrapped me up in its inebriate cotton wool and did its job. I mean, what do I care about what other people think of me? Unfortunately I do care. Oh, the joys of being human.

It's nice people feel superior when they see us. People need to feel superior when they are a slave to their jobs, their next pay packet, their HP instalment, and their haemorrhoids. Sitting there, watching people go to work and go about their daily lives, I'm learning something. What I'm learning, I'm not sure exactly. Whatever it is, it ensures that I'll always be on the bench observing it rather than participating in it.

I observe people like a train-spotter spots trains. They all look the same but they have their own numbers and little ineffectual journeys going up and down the same line. But watching people isn't very interesting; it gets boring after a while. One thing I'm certain of is that people are under the mistaken impression that they are special and extraordinary. I am under no such allusions. It is a painful truth. Life throws them at you like pins to a voodoo doll and then expects your subservience to be a happy one. I was never a happy bastard to begin with so I took the path of least resistance, which is conveniently dotted with bars and off licences.

Sometimes, though, I get all self-righteous and say I have had enough of living the loser's script. I tell myself that I am going to go from being an unemployable, law-breaking, alcoholic wanker to being an employed, law-abiding, self-respecting wanker. But when I realise that means having to get off this bench to take a piss, I think, ah, forget it. And besides, I'm just not that evil.

I'm not saying we're not annoying or smelly, but I think the reason we turn people's stomachs is that our uselessness and depravity is on show, explicit, not evil enough to be soberly and constantly held in check. And sitting on a park bench, not working, drinking and swearing, is the full extent of my evil. My evil is just not that evil, my dark side is just not that dark. There's no pretence of defence about our sins, which scares the sobers, and elicits jealousy. Because they *have* to stay sober. As alcohol obviously disinhibits, they are scared of losing control, they are petrified of showing their true selves. Behind their one thousand masks of convention and self-control, there's an evil clown wanting to make pain to laugh at – the human condition is full of strange lusts. What's the worst part of your soul? A predilection for boy scouts? An appreciation for universal tyranny and the extermination of AIDS sufferers? Auto-erotica in your mother's dress? Forget compassion and decency, apathy saves, apathy immobilises, stops a million sins and crimes in its tracks. I have a mundane lust for apathy. I hold the position of having no position. Because having a position means having to defend it, and I can't be bothered; it means taking time and energy away from drinking and rotting not so quietly, and wasting my beautiful life.

Shithead picked up a discarded paper and we scanned through it. Murmurs of disgust and criticism dribbled out of Shit's mouth. All human beings seem to retain some peculiar arrogance; it's as if you don't feel superior to something or somebody you might as well kill yourself as there doesn't seem to be any point in living otherwise.

Drunks are no better. In fact, drunks are the worst offenders. They can have two day old shit in their pants, but they think they have the answers to the world's problems. Not me, I'd rather give problems to the world's answers.

I ignored his words; he wasn't saying anything new. I simply sat there, gulping down my whiskey, waiting for a human to pass by so I could insult them. My luck was in. A whole flood of church-goers were heading our way. Our bench was strategically placed on the only accessible route between the church and the car park, which was another great thing about our bench. I spat into my palms and gleefully rubbed my hands.

I waited for the most pious-looking old bag to pass me by. Of course, she looked down her nose at me. "Awright, gorgeous," I called out to her, "I wouldn't mind smelling your cunt."

The old bag huffed, her face bloated with purple scorn. "Well, really," she sneered, "people like you should be exterminated like vermin."

Well, what a nice Christian attitude she had. Who does she and her cronies think they are? Some Sundays there are more drunks and winos on church property than church-goers. That says a lot about life. The drunks who congregate in the local churchyard are not there for the services, but for something infinitely more religious and holy. In their booze they find God every time, and the dead in the graveyard leave them alone. And, of course, the dead are even greater philosophers than the drunks. I ask the dead questions all the time – and they always give me the same answer:...........

They really know what they are saying.

Out of nowhere Shithead got up and began banging his head against a nearby tree. Shithead used to be a happy, loving, joyful child once upon a time. What happened to him? What happened to me? What has bought him to this point? How did he turn out like this? What and who is responsible? His ordinary parents and ordinary time, most likely.

"Shithead, what are you doing? Stop that!"

He stopped, and turned his head to look at me. "Wittgenstein said," said Shithead, "If you have a pre-recorded universe in which everything is pre-recorded, the only thing not pre-recorded is the pre-recordings themselves."

Shithead then dropped down dead. I cried for him and then called an ambulance, but not before I took all his money and drank all of his booze, of course.

WITHOUT A DRINK

I'm a sober nobody
who politely and quietly lets
the whole world crush me
Give me a drink however
and I'll protest *very loudly*
and tell all the nice people
of this beautiful world to
"Eff off and leave me the
hell alone."
Without a drink I'm a whore
nobody wants to fuck
but with a glass in my hand
I'm suddenly irresistible and
people can't stop fucking me over.
Without a drink I'm a person
who bloody needs one
Without a drink my conversation
is boring and vapid
lubricated with liquor, however,
I become the world's greatest
philosopher.
Without a drink
life is too painful
and I want to die.
With a drink
life is still painful
But at least I *am* dying...
... Cheers.

A LITTLE LOVE NOTE

I want to kill you
but I won't.
I will just spend
the rest of my life
hating you
with love in my heart.

IT COULD BE YOU

"Shitty fucking Christ. I don't believe this. What a bitch of a day." These curses emanated from the 22nd car stuck in a 200-car tailback on a humid Saturday night. Not only had Mac been stuck in traffic for over an hour, the hot weather was driving him crazy too. In the sickly sauna of his own skin, he was sweating like a monkey in a microwave. His day, up to that point, had been a day of average bad shite, but being stuck in a hot, sticky traffic jam disturbed the flushing mechanism of his toilet equilibrium, thereby paying the fare to set the carousel of his twisted mind in motion again. The longer he spent fixed in this putrid metal standstill, the madder he got. At one point he wanted to blow away every happy-go-lucky human being he saw. But, one: he didn't have a gun; and two: the people on the street outside were too cute for their own good. He also realised that he would merely be displacing his aggression onto innocent parties; he knew the grotesque fountainhead of his rage was himself. Reflecting upon his life always inflamed his soul. He didn't like the feeling, the presence of the soul in this day and age.

What am I doing? What the *fuck* am I doing? Why am I in a job I hate? Why am I going home to a wife that can't stand me any more? Why am I going home to children who resent me? Right now my wife will be watching one of those Saturday night game shows she loves so much. For a moment Mac was glad he was stuck in endless traffic and not sitting to his wife right now. Dazzled by the sparkling false-teethed smug smiles of game show hosts, his wife would turn to him and say, "Why can't everybody be happy like game show hosts? Why can't everybody have a smile ready for the world? Why don't you ever smile, Mac? You look handsome when you smile. I don't see you smile any more. Smile for me, Mac, please." Mac felt nauseous with his wife's request. His lips quivered uneasily before forming into a stiff smile. When his wife returned her attention to the game show on the telly, Mac dropped his smile like a lead weight and began privately entertaining thoughts of slitting the game show host's throat slowly. The smile forming on his lips wasn't so fake this time.

Another thing he had to look forward to when he got home tonight – if he ever got out of this traffic jam, that is – were more bills in the post. Plus maybe a letter or two from family members. I prefer the bills to another bloody boring letter from my mother, he sniggered to himself. Bills ask less of my soul. But he knew he was in no position to insult his mother's insipid letters of tedious wisdom. The story of his life would make boring reading too. I'm a futile and insignificant person. We are all futile and insignificant persons.

But you'd better keep hold of your sanity and that smile on your face. If you can't or don't want to take the humiliation or the loss of personal control society promises you, you're weak, inadequate. Be stronger so we can squeeze more blood out of the stone, more mileage out of you on a mediocre road going nowhere. Mac stared down the road that was going nowhere and studied the faces of other drivers: everybody looked pissed off and tense and angry; everybody was probably listening to the news on the radio right now, insulting the politicians mentioned, and cursing the injustices and tragedies of the world. Nobody really likes to adhere to rules and laws of society they think are absurd, venal and facetious, but they do it because that selfsame society provides them with the material things their little greedy hearts desire. Cars, CD systems, etc, are perfect distractions from confronting and dealing with the injustices of the world, or from asking the big questions. Example: life isn't fair, it's corrupt; those in power abuse that power blatantly; there's too much pain, etc, etc. But buying big cars and wide screen TVs ensures we keep the process going, the greedy fed, the feeble multitudes satisfied. The unscrupulous of this world don't take advantage of us, they give us what we want. We are fooled into spending obscene amounts of cash on a car with power-steering, 16 valve engine, and so on, so we can be forever stuck in traffic like this. "BUY. BUY. BUY, MOTHERFUCKER, BUY." It's in your face, it's shoved down your throat like sweetened vomit, it's everywhere – on billboards, shop windows, plastered on the sides of buses, or even on people themselves, or in the hopeful hopeless dreams behind the dead eyes of contemplating pedestrians looking for reasons to be.

One particular ad caught Mac's eye. It was the lottery ad. Here's the perfect example of what I'm talking about, thought Mac. A lot of people oppose and mistrust how the lottery charity funds are awarded; that opera houses get millions and deprived areas get nothing. But we still go out and buy more lottery tickets, turned into hypocrites through desperation. The sign says: 'IT COULD BE YOU'. And everybody's thinking, "It should be *me*, *my* pain is greater, *my* need is greater. *I* should win. *I* deserve it. And when you don't win you feel like you've been fucked over.

"After the break we have those lottery numbers coming up for you folks. Stay tuned!" The radio D.J. beamed insincerely.

Mac stayed tuned. He felt his jacket pocket for his lottery ticket; it was still there. Despite himself, Mac began to fantasise about what he'd do with the money if he won. I'd buy my kids everything they ever wished for. Maybe then they'll speak to me nicely. I'd buy my wife all the clothes she wants. Maybe then we'll love each other again. I'll buy a big mansion; it'll give us more freedom (or is it a bigger cage...).

"Here are the lottery numbers folks..." Mac fumbled for his lottery ticket and held it between his thumb and forefinger with a slight anticipatory tremor in his hand.

"The first number is 39..."

Yes, yes! I've got that.

"Next comes number 23..."

Phew, got that too!"

"41 is the next ball..."

Yes, yes. Life is beautiful. The world is as it should be. No need to get worked up over nothing. Every person is beautiful...

"The fourth ball is number 12..."

Mac felt as if he was punched in the stomach; he didn't have number 12. No matter, he told himself, I can still get five numbers and win a decent amount.

"Number 5 is next."

Number 5 was not next for Mac.

"The final number is 2..."

Mac stared at his ticket that took him halfway to heaven then dropped him from the sky without a parachute.

The traffic started moving again. But Mac did not drive home but straight into the river a few hundred metres down the road.

His suicide note was the lottery ticket pinned to his lapel.

LIFE – CHEAP AT TWICE THE PRICE

I don't know what I'm doing
or thinking any more
But then again I'm merely an incompetent
messenger in the house of pain
that is my mind: the rent is ridiculous,
but then the cheapest lives are always
The most expensive to keep.

In my darkest moments
I always see a light somewhere
something to draw me away from death.
So I apprehensively – but hopefully –
approach that light
Only to find it's somebody's death pyre,
or an illuminated sign trying to sell me
something I don't want
at an inflated price

But I have to buy it
because life is precious
and I wouldn't want to waste it now,
would I?

A DAY AT THE SEASIDE

The automatic exit doors of an anonymous seaside town railway station slide open. A man selling inflated balloons stands outside.

"Buy a balloon, luv. It'll brighten up your day. I only have a few left."

The woman who has just left the railway station shakes her head and says, "No, thank you,"

"Come on, they're for charity, for the local children's hospital."

"Okay, I'll buy one,"

The transaction takes place. The balloon seller hands her a balloon with a smiling face printed on it. "There you are, luv, one with a happy face to cheer you up. You look like you need it."

Balloon in hand, the woman walks towards the taxi rank. A cab driver sitting on the bonnet of his taxi jumps up and cheerfully greets the woman. "Want a cab?"

"Er, yes,"

"Where to?"

"The ocean, please,"

"Righto,"

Inside the taxi cab: "It's straight off to the beach for you, then?" the driver asks cordially, "Not going to book into a hotel first? Just here for the day trip?"

"Yes, I'm just here for the day," she replies unemotionally.

"Alone?"

"Yes, alone."

"No boyfriend?"

"No... not any more."

"Oh, I'm sorry about that. But there's plenty more fish in the sea... Plan to go anywhere apart from the beach?"

"No. The ocean's enough for me."

"Going for a swim?"

"You could say that."

The rest of the cab ride is silent. The smiling balloon bounces inanely about inside the cab.

The woman finds a spot on the beach and sits down. She watches the waves roll in and the waves roll out again. Seagulls devour the washed-up fish on the beach.

The woman takes off her shoes and walks down to the ocean; at the water's edge she stops. She ties the string attached to the balloon around her wrist, and walks into the ocean. A few minutes later the woman is face down in the water, dead. The smiling balloon attached to her wrist blows about in the wind.

NO LAUGHTER

No laughter for the divinity of dead clowns
Give death threats to blue skies,
name withheld, of course,
watch repeating oceans of empty mirrors,
where each sunrise has become an idyllic
defamation of the soul.
So return to your games in the playing
ground of eternal loss, while you
microwave your VD dinner
of happy uselessness.
Start what you have finished
Zero times me times the world minus
you
means nothing to me.
I'm dying to live
I'm dying to live
Start what you have finished.

SUICIDE NOTE

I just want to say...
Shit! I don't know what to say.
Life is beautiful?
I'm only killing myself
because I'm a coward?
I look out the window
and I have nothing but admiration
for those of you who have chosen
life: you look a happy, contented
bunch. Fuck, if I have to explain,
you can never know. But you do know...
... don't you?

A VERITABLE FEAST

"Come on, Jo, are you sure you don't want to go to the coast with us. It's your last chance. The car is ready to go."

"Yes, I'm sure."

"We'll stop off at a Happy Eater for lunch."

Jo shrivelled her face in disgust. "Happy Eater, huh, Happy Bulimic, more like. The Happy Eater logo has its finger down its throat, does it not? I'm not surprised, what with all that cheap, synthetic offal they serve up as food. Now I'm definitely sure I don't want to go on your trip. Besides, there's a culinary programme on TV I want to see, one that shows you what real food is."

Danielle looked at her flatmate with a sense of despair. She knew Jo would refuse to come, but she felt she had to ask. She was worried about her friend; Jo's behaviour was becoming more bizarre, reclusive and unhealthy by the day. A trip to the seaside would have done her good, get her out of her shell a bit more. Danielle had known Jo since primary school and they had been best of friends since they were 7, they did everything together. That was until a year ago. Since then, slowly but surely, Jo became more and more withdrawn, keeping herself locked in her room; when she was in the company of others, she was sullen and uncommunicative. Since losing her job, Jo spent the majority of the time furtively watching videos behind the locked door of her bedroom. Danielle was intrigued as to the contents of these secret videos. She envisioned them to be blue movies. On one of the rare days Jo went out, Danielle managed to unlock the cupboard the videos were in and slipped one into a VCR. She was disappointed to see they were nothing more than recordings of operations of various hospital documentaries. Shit, thought Danielle, why all the secrecy in watching these videos if they are not pornographic, if they are not something to be hidden?

Apart from developing strange habits, another odd dimension of her friend's new character was her sudden accident-proneness. Over the course of a few months, Jo had lost four fingers in odd circumstances. What was even stranger the accident-proneness would only manifest itself when Jo was alone. But the strangest thing of all about her accidents in the kitchen was her attitude when the paramedics arrived on the scene. She was indignant that they had been called in the first place, and the paramedics were unable to find her severed digits. Jo's explanation stunned everyone "Oh, I fed them to the dog – he looked hungry."

Jo's psychological state has definitely deteriorated, decided Danielle privately. Though paradoxically she had never seen her friend so physically fit. Jo was obsessed in keeping her body in top condition; she worked out for hours at a time. Why she was so beset in having the perfect body, Danielle had no idea. It wasn't vanity – Jo didn't flaunt her body. And it wasn't to make her more attractive to men – Jo had totally lost interest in the opposite sex. She had lost interest in humanity altogether. And she didn't keep fit for health reasons. Jo let it be known to all that she hated life and wouldn't want to live long. The only conversation people could get out of her was her caustic, bitter observations about the utter meaningless of life.

Danielle let out a sigh of resignation. She cursorily scanned the TV page of the newspaper to see what cookery programme Jo wanted to watch. "Eh?" she mouthed in puzzlement; there were no cookery programmes advertised for today whatsoever. There were the usual repeats and yet another hospital documentary. Danielle shrugged this incongruity off and left the flat to hit the road to the coast. She said goodbye to Jo; Jo stared at her old friend blankly. However, a smile formed on her face when Danielle shut the front door behind her.

Jo switched on the TV. She turned to the channel the medical documentary was on. She licked her lips as the surgeon made an incision on some poor fool's abdomen. It was at times like these Jo missed her job. She felt a slight twinge of regret.

Even though Jo had performed her duties as theatre nurse satisfactorily, the people at the hospital were glad to see the back of her. Why they did not like her was hard to pinpoint really. There was something about her demeanour that was unsettling; it was hard being in the same room as her without feeling very uncomfortable. Something about the way she looked at you, surveyed your body, seemingly with one of the deadly sins consuming her intimidating gaze. It wasn't lust exactly. Envy? No. Gluttony? Maybe...

She was also seen as untrustworthy by the hospital. She developed a reputation as being the hospital kleptomaniac. Whenever she worked in a specific hospital department, things would invariably go missing – bandages, scalpels, sutre sets, clamps, crutches, amputation saws, anaesthetic drugs. One time, en route to a transplant operation, she lost the donated organ entrusted in her keep. The oddest thing to go missing in her care were parts of research cadavers. Suspecting her of selling these spare parts to unscrupulous research laboratories, the hospital searched her bag as she left work one day, after an arm of a cadaver went missing. They found no arm in her bag or on her person. They eventually found the arm – minus its flesh, skin and sinew – stuck in a U-bend. Somebody had tried to flush it down the toilet. To avoid a scandal, and without evidence, they were reluctant to sack her for impropriety. She took her eventual dismissal for health reasons in her stride. She did love her work, but she could hardly keep her mind on the job. Whenever she assisted in intrusive surgery, it was too much for her. It was like an over-sexed teenager being the only male on a desert island of willing females... or an anorexic in a cake shop...

Not only was the local hospital her former workplace, but her supermarket, too, which was proving to be inconvenient, as she was feeling a bit peckish now.

Ah, there's no moaning about it now, Jo thought to herself. She didn't want to have to buy her food; she wanted to be totally self-sufficient. Unfortunately, because she lived in a flat, growing her own food was unrealistic. All she was able to grow were tomatoes and herbs on her balcony. Besides, she liked a bit of meat. Because of things like B.S.E. and battery hens, she gave supermarkets and butchers a wide berth. And she knew she didn't have it in her heart to raise and kill her own animals, especially if they looked up at her with pleading eyes when it was time to slaughter them. She was only capable of killing something she hated – and the only animals she hated were human beings.

Now she wasn't working in the hospital any more, she was without a means of adequate food supply, which meant it was highly impractical to eat other humans anyway. However, whenever she saw an occupied hearse trundling off to deposit its load into a hole in the ground, she admonished the waste of good food.

As her misanthropy increased, so did her distaste for consuming the people behind it. The corpses at the hospital were usually disease-ridden slabs of meat. Eating them was like eating infected, dirty offal, not unlike munching upon a cheap, tasteless burger from a fast food store – quality was definitely lacking. And why have a burger when you can have prime steak – her own body was in tip-top condition. It was also kind of like that saying: 'Every man likes the smell of his own fart.' You usually don't think twice about eating your own bogey, but the idea of eating somebody else's disgusts you.

All she had left to eat in the flat were a few shrivelled tomatoes and a few glasses of Bloody Marys in the fridge. Not only Bloody Marys, but bloody Johns, stupid Sarahs, and an irksome Mr Johnson – names suspiciously similar to those on the blood donor register.

She downed a few glasses but still wasn't satisfied. Her over-riding urge to devour herself was growing with every growl of her empty stomach. Maybe it's better to surrender to this impulse to self-cannibalise. What's the alternative? Struggling financially, mentally, emotionally from day to day for the sake of a beautiful life.

The world was tearing her apart, piece by piece, she could definitely feel the world around her slowly and insidiously consume her being. Why can't I have my share of the cake? Jo asked herself with some degree of exasperation and indignation. It was an act of ultimate self-control – to devour yourself before the rest of the world does.

Apart from that, her body was in constant pain anyway. Tests were carried out but no cause was found. "It's all in your head," her G.P. smirked disdainfully, "psychosomatic." Which meant she had to find her own cure: painkillers did not kill the pain; faith-healers did not heal; acupuncture merely made holes. The only way she would not feel pain was if there was no body to feel the pain. Self-mutilation did not go deep enough for Jo. I not merely content to cut the skin on my arm – I want to saw the damn arm off. I want to gorge my eyes out. I want to extract my teeth with a smile on my face. I want to pour my brain into a blender and drink its juices of rank and tainted ineptitude, Jo asserted forcefully. She was finally ready to shed the futile and profitless – yet delicious – cocoon that was her body.

Jo spread out her array of surgical instruments purposefully. She injected herself with a local anaesthetic in the appropriate regions of her body; when it took effect, she made a deep incision into her left arm at her elbow, cutting through connective tissues. Her job gave her the technical skill to perform the intricate amputation of her left arm. After completing the job and sewing herself up, she ground the flesh of her amputated arm through a mincer and made spaghetti Bolognese with the meat, along with tomatoes, herbs, and a packet of spaghetti past its sell-by date lurking forlornly in the back of an extremely bare food cupboard.

She savoured the thought, as her body digested her own body, that her being was being transformed into shit. How appropriate. What a suitable and befitting fate.

Continuing with her self-dismemberment, her right leg was next to come off; she gormandised it from the top of the thigh down, stopping short at her ankles. Feet, yuk, I can't eat my own feet, Jo whined to herself. She could hear her mother say out loud in her head, "You were always a fussy eater."

However, she did stuff her face with her own face, and ate and drank to her heart's content. Actually, she did drink her heart's content. Needless to say, despite the anaesthetic and careful surgical procedures, the pain was too much, and the blood loss too great: her circulation collapsed and she went into shock. Death came quickly. If she hadn't eaten her own lips, there would have been a smile of contentment on her face.

NOTHING ON THE MENU

A dingy, anonymous café:
cups of coffee, sunlight
on the spoons, on worn-down
tables, chairs, on
worn-down people.
The neon flashes
'Hungry?'
in the window

During a quiet period,
The waitress looks out of the window
Fifteen years of waitressing... shit
Fifteen years of tasting grease in everything
Fifteen years of washing endless dirty dishes
Fifteen years of endless dirty old men smiles
Fifteen years of lewd comments, of being leered at
Fifteen years of politely, coldly letting them.
As she got older, it happened less and less
until they finally ignored her.
She didn't know which she preferred

"I want to die, I want to die, I want to die,"
she'd repeat as a mantra – it helped her to
get through the day.
She realised her life to come would be the same
as her life before: no new loves, no new
experiences, no new thoughts, no new
answers to the big questions, like:
What is the meaning of life?
And is it precious?
It must be if it is so expensive to live it.
And the biggest question of them all:
The sign outside states this is Joe's Café
But who the hell is Joe?

A DAY OUT IN THE PARK

The sun shines. The park flowers are blooming majestically – the day couldn't be more perfect. It's Sunday. Quality time. Picnics. Sunbathers. Happy families. Dripping ice cream cones. Dogs energetically chase sticks and balls. Kites contend with the birds for the skies.

An ordinary-looking man leans against a tree stump, watching all this with a smile on his face. It's the perfect setting for him. Life isn't so bad when it's like this. Even the bees landing on his skin don't bother him. A little girl, having picked some flowers, disengages herself from her family strolling along a path to hand him a bunch of daisies. "Here you are, Mister,"

He grins playfully at the little girl. "Why, thank you, sweetheart. They're lovely."

The little girl giggles bashfully and runs back to join her family. She turns around to say goodbye to him. He waves back, pulling a funny face to make her laugh.

The man opens his canvas tool bag and pulls out a ham sandwich. A passing dog takes an interest in the ham. The man tears off a piece of sandwich and tosses it into the waiting jaws of the hopeful canine, slobbering with anticipation. The dog totters off with a wag in its tail.

A few beautiful women pass him by. He smiles at them. Sometimes he gets a smile back. He delves into his tool bag and pulls out the last item in it. He rises to his feet.

He smiles once again. The machine gun in his hand massacres seventeen people in the park in less than half a minute.

The beautiful sun in the skies stays beautiful.

TAKE IT IN YOUR STRIDE

I do a lot of walking, journeys without destinations,
all the places I pass are mere way stations
to our beautiful eventual nothingness.
On one of these walks I witnessed an armed robbery:
        A security guard got shot in the face; he died instantly
That's funny, I thought. I don't mean funny
as in ha, ha – nobody was laughing.
I thought it was funny that only a few minutes before
the security guard was thinking his boring, ordinary
thoughts, and worrying about his bills, and
pondering what to watch on TV that night.
In all likelihood he wasn't a happy man, and to
top it all off, his starchy uniform was chaffing
him raw on this hot summery day. It's funny
that one moment he was feeling like hell, and then
-    BANG! – he was dead, wiped clean
from existence, extinguished.
At that precise moment his wife was probably
watching a daytime game show; she has no idea
he's dead now. That's strange, very strange indeed.
Then I was hit by a horrible thought:
An awful, anonymous life is better than no
life at all – that's the tragedy.
But his kids will still cry for him
and miss him very much.
I walk away and try not to think about it.
But I do.

NATURAL

I love nature
She's a beautiful goddess
and evil bitch, all rolled
into one sun, one moon,
one earth.
She constantly screams,
"There's too many bloody people!"
So as a form of population control,
she gives us the gifts of disease,
famine, drought, hurricanes,
earthquakes and fire.
But still she screams,
"There's too many bloody people!
And they are chewing on my brain
like maggots!"
We've turned nature into a brain-dead
homicidal
cosmic
non-entity.
But still the sun shines.

LOVE'S FINAL NOTICE

The sunlight slowly washed over the ground I found myself sleeping on. My body was stiff from sleeping on alleyway concrete, and my palate still retained the flavour of last night's nausea. I wasn't sick this morning, though – not physically anyway. Yesterday had been my job interview. I hate job interviews more than I hate doing the actual job. It means coming up with disgustingly happy reasons why you want to surrender your soul to some form of spurious, bland servility. I can't do it without either wanting to kill myself or piss myself with laughter. Yesterday was no exception. Midway through telling a personnel manager why it was my ambition to work in a toilet roll factory, I stopped reading from the bad script of the bad play society had concocted, and vomited all over his desk. The faltering interview was effectively over at that moment. Without even bothering to apologise, I just got up and left.

Now the D.S.S. would be stopping my dole money for sure. Puking over the personnel manager's desk was worse than not turning up for the interview. But I no longer cared. I had enough money in my pocket to get drunk and 1001 ways to commit suicide in this fair city. So last night I got drunk – but ended up too tired and sick to kill myself.

My agenda for today was to consume vast amounts of alcohol for breakfast, and then commit anonymous suicide for lunch. I sat up and examined myself. I still had my life, still had money in my pocket, and I still had my knickers on. So it was obvious I hadn't been murdered, robbed or raped during my alleyway sleep. Humanity was evidently in a benevolent mood last night. Or maybe they just couldn't find me – the alleyway was a good hiding place. I got up onto my unsteady feet and, with my hangover guiding my steps, I made my way to a public convenience.

At a public convenience sink I washed myself as best as I could. The taste in my mouth was ugly. So I gargled with water and chewed my last stick of chewing gum to freshen up my breath. Then I washed myself with warm water and sticky dispenser soap. It was at this point I got into an argument with the lavatory attendant. She told me I wasn't allowed to wash myself at the sink – it was only for hands. "Where am I supposed to wash, then – in the toilet?" I retorted. "Why is it your problem? I'm not going to leave a mess behind. You won't even know I've been here." This was a blatant and obvious lie. But I couldn't placate the old cow. She seemed to be drowning in a permanent black mood. But then wouldn't you be the same if you worked for less than the recommended minimum wage and had to clean after people unable to shit into the actual toilet. I felt bad. So apologised, cleared up, and left.

Once outside, I got rid of my coat. It was dirty and advertised too many of last night's deadly sins, such as sloth, lust and gluttony. The morning was chilly, but my long walk to Soho, where I knew some illegal all-night bars operated, would warm me up.

I sat myself at the end of the bar. It was on top of a sex shop, so there were the obligatory dirty old men drinking upstairs as well. If the porno mags downstairs couldn't lift their, erm, souls, overpriced alcohol would. A few tried to hit on me – they thought I was some over-sexed housewife. And, of course, they were right. But I wasn't interested in thirty second intercourse. Why fucking bother? I'd get more passion, love and attention out of a vibrator.

But their hard-ons soon changed directions. Another woman entered the bar. I couldn't blame them – she was absolutely beautiful. Don't make me describe her physical attributes here on the page, I won't be able to take it. Two fucking days after splitting up with her, I am trying to write objectively the story of how we met, after three acrimonious years together. Our love finally became ugly, hurtful, so what's the use of bringing beauty into the story. The gun next to this computer doesn't need any more excuses to be used.

Back to the story however...

Despite their hard-ons and fat butts, the men in the bar suddenly found room next to themselves for her to sit.

But she sat next to me.

When it was obvious they were going to have more luck with the rubber dolls downstairs, the male clientele of the bar soon left to return to their unhappy jobs and even unhappier wives.

The summer sun hadn't totally eradicated the unsunned ring mark of her wedding finger. I spotted this as I indulgently savoured her being as she drained drink after drink.

"You want another drink?" I finally had the courage to ask her.

"That's a stupid question, isn't it?"

"I guess it is," I ordered more drinks for myself and Sara. "Just got divorced, huh?" I always say the wrong things, ask the wrong questions. My conversational skills aren't well developed. But then again I've never had anything worth saying.

Sara rubbed the pale shadow of her discarded ring. "Yes, I've just got divorced. What about you – are you married?"

"No, I've never been married. Been divorced plenty of times, though."

"Eh? Well, my husband, I mean my ex-husband wanted me to stop drinking and become a dutiful wife."

"So you divorced on the grounds of mental cruelty?"

"You could say that. He said my drinking was driving us apart. I had to disagree with him – it was what kept us together."

"Why's that, then?"

"There's one thing I'm grateful to my alcoholism for."

"What's that, then?"

"Heterosexuality."

So that was how we met. After, we went to her flat to make love. I postponed my suicide. I decided to take the slow way out – love.

Why am I writing about how we met now that we are no longer together? Because the best suicide notes are love stories – and vice versa. Well, this first chapter will be the last. I can't go on any more – with life or this fucking story.

So here is the final chapter.

BROKEN

A dripping tap can drive U insane
Like your own heart beating to
a rhythm you can't adjust to.
Yes, my heart is a faucet
losing itself drop by drop, silently
in its own corner
Just making enough noise
to annoy whoever is listening.
Drip – a liquid discard of soul in instalments
Drop – all day
Drip – every day.

STREET SATORI

Pausing in my step
I saw something beautiful
The people who shared
the pavement with me hated
my existence in an instant
without even knowing me
cursing me for slowing down
their great, important
worthy journeys. I stepped
aside and let them go
Let them be with their own
coveted uselessness.
I looked down, by my feet:
The sun was shining
into a puddle,
and raindrops were giving me
a thousand variations of
Cosmic beauty.
Was I the only person to see it?
Why is that?
Because it doesn't pay the bills,
so let's chuck it out.
I'm glad I look through other
people's rubbish then.

ELEVATION

"You know how to press my buttons," he snarled.
"Why don't you press mine," I told him. "I have
a million floors of self-loathing, disgust, love
and sunshine... Jump from any story you want.
I've got loads of them too.
You're stuck between floors
Stuck in the lift with me, and the piss and shit
of those before us.
There's nothing to do but screw our brains out
and wait for elevation."

PROZAC WHORE

I'm a Prozac whore
An existence bore
A rotting fruit of knowledge core
The perfect flaw
The dead bird soar
But mostly I'm a Prozac whore
I'm chemically delirious
I'm so happy I could take
the whole bottle
Suicide is a toilet
I won't flush
Death is a thing I won't rush
Tattoo smiley faces
on my scars
Show the world that I'm
Happy, trigger happy
Let me fulfil my agenda
of inconsequence
Living for every new day
that comes
ejaculating prematurely
into the void
I love the sun
but hate the day it brings
like a bad aftertaste
So sun
I will rise high enough
To shoot you down
One day
One day.

EATEN MIRROR

I seem to monopolise the psychic bureaucracy of stupidity
So douse my pain in bleach
Drown my laughter with gasoline
My eyes take pictures I wish I could tear up
Life is a two-dimensional pain, an
eaten mirror where snakes swim in my brain
I'm going to commit suicide on my birthday
It's the best present life has ever given me
When I go to hell, I'll say hi to the devil for you

GOD'S SUICIDE NOTE

I'm God
I hate my fucking job
Do you want it?
Even the devil wouldn't have me
I created billions of minions
to bow down before me
But not one will suck my dick
except this leery witch called Mary,
who wants child support
payments for eternity,
the bitch.

I said do not eat from the tree
of knowledge. I wanted humans
to be dumb sacks of shit. It
made me feel good or something.

I remember one angelic fucker
took me, God, hostage.
He sodomised me, the bastard,
and then he said, "You created
everything here, God."

So on the eighth day, God surveyed
everything around him and said,
"What the hell have I done?... Shit...
Goodbye cruel world..."
And committed suicide.

It was heavenly.

WRITE YOUR OWN SUICIDE NOTE HERE:

NOW TEAR THE FUCKING THING UP!

**CHECK OUT MORE GREAT TITLES AT
www.holebooks.co.uk**

**To get deeper into underground writing
enter the hole**